JINNAH S.

GAME BOY®

SECRET
CODES

3

||||||BRADYGAMES
TAKE YOUR GAME FURTHER™

GAME BOY® SECRET CODES 3

©2001 Pearson Education

BradyGAMES® is a registered trademark of Pearson Education, Inc.

BradyGAMES®

An Imprint of Pearson Education
201 West 103rd Street
Indianapolis, Indiana 46290

Game Boy® and Game Boy® Advance are registered trademarks of Nintendo of America Inc. TM, ® and "N" logo are trademarks of Nintendo of America Inc. All rights reserved.

Please be advised that the ESRB rating icons, "EC", "K-A", "T", "M", and "AO" are copyrighted works and certification marks owned by the Interactive Digital Software Association and the Entertainment Software Rating Board and may only be used with their permission and authority. Under no circumstances may the rating icons be self-applied to any product that has not been rated by the ESRB. For information regarding whether a product has been rated by the ESRB, please call the ESRB at (212) 759-0700 or 1-800-771-3772. Please note that ESRB ratings only apply to the content of the game itself and do NOT apply to the content of the books.

ISBN: 0-7440-0085-8

Library of Congress Catalog No.: 2001-132512

Printing Code: The rightmost double-digit number is the year of the book's printing; the rightmost single-digit number is the number of the book's printing. For example, 01-1 shows that the first printing of the book occurred in 2001.

04 03 02 01   4 3 2 1

Manufactured in the United States of America.

BRADYGAMES STAFF

Director of Publishing
David Waybright

Editor-In-Chief
H. Leigh Davis

Creative Director
Robin Lasek

Marketing Manager
Janet Eshenour

Licensing Assistant
Mike Degler

Assistant Marketing Manager
Susie Nieman

Nintendo Title Manager
Tim Fitzpatrick

CREDITS

Senior Project Editor
David B. Bartley

Screenshot/Development Editor
Michael Owen

Designer
Kurt Owens

Production Designer
Tracy Wehmeyer

ACKNOWLEDGMENTS

BradyGAMES would like to sincerely thank everyone at Nintendo of America, especially Cammy Budd, Juana Tingdale, Joy Ashizawa, and the entire NOA Testing Group. Your generous assistance helped make this guide possible—thank you!

THE GAMES

THE GAMES

THE GAMES

GAME BOY® LEGEND

ABBREV.	WHAT IT MEANS
Left	Left on + Control Pad
Right	Right on + Control Pad
Up	Up on + Control Pad
Down	Down on + Control Pad
START	Press START
SELECT	Press SELECT
A	Press A Button
B	Press B Button

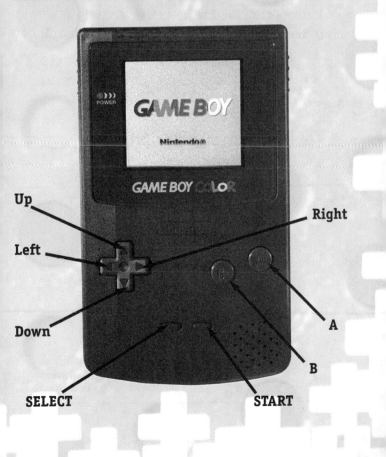

102 DALMATIANS: PUPPIES TO THE RESCUE

GARAGE LEVEL

Enter **BONE, BONE, PAWPRINT, TANK** as a password.

CAFETERIA LEVEL

Enter **DOMINO, BONE, KEY, PAW PRINT** as a password.

CRUELLA - FINAL LEVEL

Enter **TOY, BONE, BONE, BONE** as a password.

1942

PASSWORDS

STAGE	PASSWORD
04	Medal, Medal, Your Plane, Enemy Plane

08	Your Plane, Enemy Plane, Enemy Plane, Medal

12	Bullet, Enemy Plane, Your Plane, Your Plane
16	Enemy Plane, Enemy Plane, Bullet, Enemy Plane
20	Your Plane, Medal, Bullet, Your Plane
24	Bullet, Your Plane, Medal, Medal
28	Medal, Enemy Plane, Medal, Enemy Plane

ACTION MAN

ACCESS ALL LEVELS

Enter **7!B!** as a password.

ARMY MEN

PASSWORDS

LEVEL	PASSWORD
2	Grenade, Machine Gun, Helicopter, Jeep
3	Jeep, Helicopter, Helicopter, Jeep
4	Gun, Grenade, Gun, Grenade

ARMY MEN 2

ALL FIELD AND ASSUALT LEVELS

Enter **Helicopter, Jeep, Grenade, Rifle** as a password.

ARMY MEN: AIR COMBAT

PASSWORDS

LEVEL	PASSWORD
2	Crate, Cross, Crate, Crate
3	Missile, Missile, Missile, Cross
4	Insignia, Missile, Crate, Crate
5	Cross, Insignia, Cross, Missile
6	Helmet, Missile, Insignia, Helmet
7	Crate, Cross, Missile, Cross
8	Missile, Insignia, Cross, Helmet
9	Insignia, Insignia, Missile, Missile
10	Cross, Helmet, Cross, Helmet
11	Helmet, Insignia, Cross, Helmet
12	Crate, Cross, Insignia, Insignia
13	Missile, Cross, Helmet, Helmet
14	Insignia, Crate, Cross, Insignia
15	Cross, Crate, Insignia, Helmet
16	Helmet, Cross, Missile, Insignia

ARMY MEN: SARGE'S HEROES 2

PASSWORDS

MISSION	PASSWORD
1	P2Z7Q4LB
2	C1F6Q3TP
3	V4R2B1JK
4	X6K2L1KT
5	S5H8L2RG
6	Y2C3T6BF
7	F1C4P9VP
8	VJC2PFHC
9	W3S4C75S
10	M8R2X4LS
11	KBHD4V1D
12	14NN6168
13	PDO1S4N5
14	B0T7V9CK
15	BDD61977
16	K4TLLC11
17	S6P8D2KG
18	77N5Y14N
19	Y2K4X8TP
20	825VN1N6
21	KFH1JGCO
22	T3F8R0ZY
23	Y7C8R2N0
24	XW3L7B26
25	C2X3Q5TC
26	LV75HRR9
27	D2K7POS4

CONTINUED

28	H4KXJ68D
29	1NSY1912
30	JYMCBB01

ASTERIX: SEARCH FOR DOGMATIX

PASSWORDS

AREA	PASSWORD
Lutetia	CQPSJ
Massilia	MLSPS
Alexandria	RSFMS
Memphis	TPPGN

Memphis

ASTEROIDS

CHEAT MENU

To enter the Cheat Menu, enter **CHEATONX** as your password, then press **SELECT** to enter the menu.

Cheat Menu

| Level Select: Up or Down |
| Zone Select: Left or Right |
| The A Button toggles Invincibility |

PASSWORDS

ZONE	PASSWORD
Zone 2	SPACEVAC
Zone 3	STARSBRN
Zone 4	WORMSIGN
Zone 5	INCOMING

CLASSIC ASTEROIDS

Enter **QRTREATR** as your password for the original '70s version of the game.

Classic Asteroids

CONTINUED

UNLOCK SECRET "EXCALIBUR" SPACESHIP

Enter **PROJECTX** as your password for the secret ship.

Excalibur

AUSTIN POWERS: OH BEHAVE!

FAB-DOS CODES

Type the following in FAB-DOS:

TYPE...	UNLOCK...
CCTV	'Ivana...' wallpaper
CHRISTMAS	'Flowers & Evil' screen saver
DOG	'Swallow's eye' wallpaper
GET YOU	'Get You' sound

| GRACE | 'Moving Logos' screen saver |
| HANDS | 'Driving' wallpaper |

IDIOT	'Nerd Alert' sound
JUMBO	'Jet Rockin' sound
LOOK	'Foxy Felicity' wallpaper
MAGPIE	'Maggie' sound
NO MOJO	'Lost Mojo' sound
RAT POISON	Invincible in Platform game
SPACE	'Bust an O-Ring' wallpaper
SPEEDY	Faster in Maze game
SPRINGER	'Elvis lives!' wallpaper
STEIN	'Fembot Vanessa' wallpaper
TEARS	'Hands Up!" wallpaper
TEETHING	'Austin steam' wallpaper
TWO OF US	'Sausages' wallpaper

CONTINUED

HIDDEN MESSAGES

Enter the following in FAB-DOS to get hidden messages:

SHAG	HORNY
SHAGADELIC	RANDY

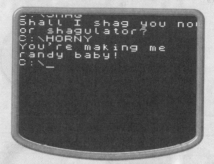

AUSTIN POWERS: WELCOME TO MY UNDERGROUND LAIR!

EVIL-DOS CODES

Type the following in EVIL-DOS:

TYPE...	UNLOCK...
125CC	Faster in Mojo Maze
ANOTHER PLAN	'Plan 2' sound
BANGERS	'Evil & Mini-Me' wallpaper
CHRISTMAS	'Flowers & Evil' screen saver
DOCTOR	'Evil Dr' sound
DRIVING	'Mini-Me Hands' wallpaper
ELVIS	'Springer Evil' wallpaper
FOXY	'Evil Look' wallpaper

GRACE	'Moving Logos' screen saver
HUG	'Hug' sound
INVINCIBLE	Infinite Lives in Mojo Maze
IVANA YUM	'Evil CCTV' wallpaper
MINI LAUGH	'Mini-Me Hehehe' sound
OIL RING	'Mini-me in space' wallpaper
STEAM	'Teething' wallpaper

STICKUP	'Evil Tears' wallpaper
SUPERVISOR	'The Boss' sound
SWALLOW	'Alpha-Dog' wallpaper
TABLE	'Table Problem' sound
TASTY FEMBOT	'Evil-Stein' wallpaper

HIDDEN MESSAGES

Enter the following in EVIL-DOS to get hidden messages:

LASER   BIGGLESWORTH   MOJO

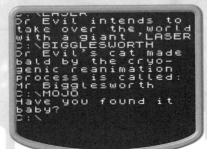

AZURE DREAMS

CAPTURE RARE MONSTERS

Use an Ovaseed to capture Guardians and Souvenirs. Throw it at the monsters to catch them.

BABE AND FRIENDS

LEVEL PASSWORDS

LEVEL	PASSWORD
02	BOB
03	RN6
04	G5M
05	RM1
06	N6W
07	TYQ

Level 07

BATMAN: CHAOS IN GOTHAM

PASSWORDS

LEVEL	PASSWORD
2	Batman, Batmobile, Batman, Batcycle
3	Batman, Batcycle, Batgirl, Batcycle
4	Batmobile, Batmobile, Batman, Batmobile
5	Batmobile, Batcycle, Batgirl, Batgirl
6	Batcycle, Batcycle, Batman, Batgirl
7	Batcycle, Batgirl, Batgirl, Batman
8	Batgirl, Batcycle, Batman, Batmobile
9	Batgirl, Batgirl, Batmobile, Batcycle

BEATMANIA GB2: GOTCHA MIX

ALL SONGS

Enter **YEBISUSAMA** as a password.

CONTINUED

SONG PASSWORDS

SONG	PASSWORD
Friends	MELODIOUS
Rydeen	GROOVY
Ultraman's Song	SUPERCOOL
Genom Screams	WONDERFUL
Watashiga	SPLENDID

BILLY BOB'S HUNTIN' 'N' FISHIN'

HUNT TURKEY AND PIKE

Enter **Pig, Boat, Bag, Deer, Bag, Deer** as a password.

BLADE

GAME ENDING

Enter **9?!1N?BKT?51G** as a password.

BLASTER MASTER: ENEMY BELOW

LEVEL SELECT CODES

LEVEL	CODE
1	E6C3D3KF
2	E6D3D3KG
3	E7C3D3KH
4	E7D3D3KI
5	F6C3D3KQ
6	F6D3D3KR
7	F7C3D3KU
8	F7D3D3KT

BOARDER ZONE

BONUS TRACK

Enter **020971** as a password.

LEVEL 4 & 5 TRICK ATTACK

Enter **290771** as a password. Levels 4 and 5 will now be available in Challenge mode.

BOMBERMAN MAX BLUE: CHAMPION

LOCATIONS OF CHARABOMS

Shell:	1-10
Pommy:	1-1
Seadran:	2-2
Panther Fang:	2-10
Beast Pommy:	3-3
Sea Balloon:	3-10
Puteladon:	4-4
Unicornos:	4-9
Iron Squid:	5-8
Animal Pommy:	5-15

CHARABOM COMBINATIONS

Aqua Dragon = Fire + Water

Pommy Dragon = Fire + Electric

Thunder Kong = Earth + Electric

Thunder Shark = Water + Electric

Rock Snakey = Water + Earth

A
B
C
D
E
F
G
H
I
J
K
L
M
N
O
P
Q
R
S
T
U
V
W
X
Y
Z

BOMBERMAN MAX RED: CHAMPION

CHARABOM LOCATIONS

Draco:	1-1
Elephant:	1-10
Marine Eel:	2-2
Knuckle Pommy:	2-10
Twin Dragon:	3-10
Big Ox:	3-3
Sharkin:	4-4
Hammer Pommy:	4-9
Iron Dragon:	5-8
Mecha Kong:	5-15

CHARABOM COMBINATIONS

Aqua Dragon = Fire + Water

Pommy Dragon = Fire + Electric

Thunder Kong = Earth + Electric

Thunder Shark = Water + Electric

Rock Snakey = Water + Earth

Fire Force = Fire + Earth

BUFFY THE VAMPIRE SLAYER

PASSWORDS

LEVEL	PASSWORD
1	3NKFZ8
2	9MD1WV
3	XTN4F7
4	5BVPL2
5	9D6F0S
6	TSCNB4
7	CSJTQZ
8	BNPXZ9

BUGS BUNNY CRAZY CASTLE 4

PASSWORDS

STAGE	PASSWORD
1-2	RHY043
1-3	HDY04?
1-4	7DY04Z
1-5	KQM04X
2-1	76504X
2-2	?GP04Z
2-3	TDP04X
2-4	KNYS4V
2-5	TQCS34
3-1	1DFS35
3-2	9DFS33
3-3	?Q5S34
4-1	T45934
4-2	?XP83Z
4-3	RD5S3?
4-4	F4Y034
4-5	34Y032
5-1	WZY034
5-2	3GY030
5-3	WNP03Z
5-4	56303T
5-5	FZMJ24
6-1	5GM03T
6-2	W6WS3V
6-3	P6CS26
7-1	PGCS22
7-2	FQMS24

CONTINUED

A
C
D
E
F
G
H
I
J
K
L
M
N
O
P
Q
R
S
T
U
V
W
X
Y
Z

STAGE	PASSWORD
7-3	M4PS27
7-4	WD5S20
7-5	3DPS22
7-6	H0F02?
8-1	70Y022
8-2	?8Y020
8-3	7SY020
8-4	HJP02Y
8-5	70P02Z
8-6	18P02Y
9-1	PSPJ15
9-2	H0FS17
9-3	72Y814
9-4	KSFS16
9-5	RSFS15
9-6	K0PS25
10-1	RJ5S11
10-2	1B3S1?
10-3	TB3S1Z
10-4	YLW011
10-5	PLW010
10-6	FBC01V
10-7	3BC01S
10-8	W2M01Z
11-1	P0M01X
11-2	W53006
11-3	MSM01T
11-4	F0CS04
11-5	MJCS04
11-6	WSW80Z
11-7	38FS02

STAGE	PASSWORD
11-8	F2M8OZ
12-1	PL3SOO
12-2	CSPSO5
12-3	5V3SO?
12-4	KQROOO
12-5	R6RJOT
12-6	1DTOO1
12-7	TD9OOX
12-8	H4KJ?7
13-1	R4KJ?7

BURAI FIGHTER (GBC)

LEVEL PASSWORDS

LEVEL	EAGLE	ALBATROSS	ACE
2	BRFG	NKMR	KDMT
3	KTDC	TCKP	SNNS
4	DRMF	NQTK	KMGT
5	SRSD	MQFH	MSKD

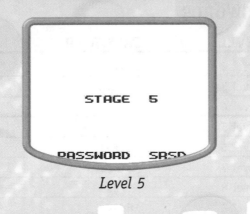

STAGE 5

PASSWORD SRSD

Level 5

BUZZ LIGHTYEAR OF STAR COMMAND

PASSWORDS

LEVEL	PASSWORDS
2	BBVBB
3	CVVBB
4	XBVBB
5	YVVBB
6	GBVBB
7	HVVBB
8	3BVBB
9	4VVBB
10	LBVBB
11	MVVBB
12	7BVBB
13	8VVBB

CATWOMAN

PASSWORDS

LEVEL	PASSWORD
Level 2	K6T@1
Level 3	1QT@@
Level 4	KQYXY
Level 5	1@FVQ
Level 6	K@FVP
Level 7	@JFV4
Level 8	KJFZR
Level 9	16TJV

CHICKEN RUN

INVISIBILITY

Enter **Crown, Bronze, Honor, Valor** as a password.

STAGE SKIP

Enter **Honor, Valor, Bronze, Silver** as a password. Pause the game and press **SELECT** to skip to the next stage.

UNLIMITED TIME

Enter **Diamond, Honor, Cross, Crown** as a password.

PASSWORDS

LEVEL	PASSWORD
2	Bronze, Cross, Crown, Bravery
3	Diamond, Bravery, Honor, Bronze
4	Cross, Bravery, Bronze, Bronze
5	Crown, Diamond, Crown, Honor
6	Valor, Diamond, Cross, Silver

CONKER'S POCKET TALES

RESTORE HEALTH

Save the game when you're low on health, then load your saved game. Your health should now be full.

A
B
C
D
E
F
G
H
I
J
K
L
M
N
O
P
Q
R
S
T
U
V
W
X
Y
Z

DAVE MIRRA FREESTYLE BMX

FULL GAME

Enter **R6KZBS7L1CTQMH** as a password.

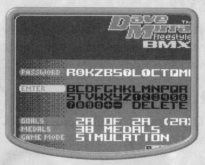

Full Game

DONALD DUCK: GOIN' QUACKERS

PASSWORDS

LEVEL	PASSWORD
1-2	YMPHTM9
1-3	VNQJVPY
1-4	2ZSLXSW
1-5	PWYR3XD
2-1	1KC71PL

DRIVER

ACCESS THE CHEAT MENU

At the Main Menu screen, enter in the following code to unlock the Cheat Menu.

Highlight "Undercover" and press **UP, UP, DOWN, DOWN, UP, DOWN, UP, DOWN, UP, UP, DOWN, DOWN.** If you entered the code correctly, the Cheats Menu option will become available. Access the Cheats Menu and turn ON or OFF any of the options by pressing **RIGHT** to activate them or pressing **LEFT** to deactivate them.

LEVEL PASSWORDS

LEVEL	PASSWORDS
1	Face, Face, Face, Face
2	Tire Mark, Badge, Cone, Red Siren
3	Stop Light, Key, Key, Blue Siren
4	Cone, Cone, Cone, Badge
5	Key, Red Siren, Siren, Stoplight
6	Key, Badge, Tire Mark, Blue Siren
7	Badge, Cone, Badge, Red Siren
8	Red Siren, Badge, Key, Tire Tread
9	Cone, Blue Siren, Red Siren, Red Siren
10	Badge, Badge, Stoplight, Cone
11	Blue Siren, Key, Key, Key
12	Stoplight, Tire Tread, Red Siren, Badge
13	Key, Badge, Badge, Cone
14	Red Siren, Blue Siren, Red Siren, Blue Siren
15	Tire Tread, Key, Cone, Stoplight

DUKE NUKEM

LEVEL SELECT

At the "Press Start" screen, press **Left, Right, Up, Up, Down, Up, Right, Left.**

Level Select

INVINCIBILITY

At the "Press Start" screen, press **Up, Down, Down, Left, Right, Left, Up, Up.** You should hear a noise if you enter the code correctly.

EARTHWORM JIM: MENACE 2 THE GALAXY

UNLOCK LEVEL 4

Enter the following passwords at the Password screen:

3bdnkg
3bbbbb
bb3hbl

GRAVEYARD

Enter the following passwords at the Password screen:

LYBBBB

BBBBBB

BBBBLY

UNLOCK ALL LEVELS

Enter the following passwords at the Password screen:

EBDNKG

3BBBBB

BB3HBL

ECW: HARDCORE REVOLUTION

RAVEN'S PASSWORDS

Enter in the following passwords to access Raven's career.

CAREER	PASSWORD
1 win	qchmhhfg
3 wins	Sfkpkkcj
4 wins	Mgbqbbjc
5 wins	Lhcacckb
6 wins	Pjdsddgf
7 wins	Nkfhfhd
8 wins	Hlqbqqna
9 wins	Gmacaapq
10 wins & TV Title	Knsdsslt
11 wins & TV Title	Jptfttms

CONTINUED

CAREER	PASSWORD
13 wins & TV Title	Brmhmmtl
14 wins & TV Title	Fsnjnnqp
15 wins & TV Title	Dtpkpprn
16 wins & TV Title	Rlglggdh
17 wins & TV Title	Qmhmhhfg

FIFA 2000

LEVEL	PASSWORDS
2	SDLSNP
3	DCDWTP
4	SPLGZW
5	DQRFKW
6	PSQQLW
7	NBGJVX

FORCE 21

MISSION PASSWORDS

MISSION	PASSWORD
2	LXCR
3	PTKL
4	LSGY
5	DUSM

FROGGER

CHEAT MODE

After losing all of your lives, press **A, B, SELECT, START** at the High Score screen.

STOP TRAFFIC AND TURTLES.

Press **A, B, B, Left, Right, Up, B, A** during gameplay. If you do this properly, a traffic light should appear and stop all traffic, and turtles will no longer dive underwater.

GEX 3: DEEP POCKET GECKO

MYSTERY TV STATUS

Enter **4BFBBBM329BBBBBBBB** as a password.

GRAND THEFT AUTO

LEVEL SELECT

Name your character **LEVELS** or **WENDY.**

HIDDEN CHARACTERS

Name your character **KELLY** or **SUMNER.**

HALLOWEEN RACER

ADVANCED LEVEL

Enter **2!!MT9** as a password.

A
B
C
D
E
F
G
H
I
J
K
L
M
N
O
P
Q
R
S
T
U
V
W
X
Y
Z

HOT WHEELS STUNT TRACK DRIVER

UNLOCK ALL CARS AND TRACKS

Enter **Down, Left, Up, A, Down, Right** as a password.

LEVEL PASSWORDS FOR SHADOW JET

LEVEL	PASSWORD
2	Left, Up, Left, Down, Up, A
3	Right, Up, Right, Down, Up, A
4	Up, B, Up, Up, Left, A
5	B, Left, B, Up, Up, Left
6	Down, Left, Up, A, Up, Up
End	Down, Left, Up, A, Down, Right

LEVEL PASSWORDS FOR SLIDE OUT

LEVEL	PASSWORD
2	Down, A, Up, A, B, B
3	Left, B, Left, Right, Down, B
4	Down, B, B, B, Right, Down
5	A, A, Right, Right, B, Down
6	Right, Up, Left, Up, Left, Right
End	Down, Left, Up, A, Down, Right

LEVEL PASSWORDS FOR TOE JAM

LEVEL	PASSWORD
2	B, B, Left, Up, A, B
3	Left, Left, Up, A, Right, Right
4	Left, Left, Up, Left, A, Left
5	Down, Up, Left, Down, Down, A
6	B, B, B, Right, Right, Up
End	Down, Left, Up, A, Down, Right

LEVEL PASSWORDS FOR TWIN MILL

Twin Mill Passwords

LEVEL	PASSWORD
2	Down, Left, B, B, Right, B
3	Up, B, Down, Down, Right, Left
4	Right, Up, Right, D, D, Right
5	Right, Up, Right, Down, A, Right
6	Right, Left, Up, A, Up, Down
End	Down, Left, Up, A, Down, Right

LEVEL PASSWORDS FOR WAY TOO FAST

Way Too Fast Passwords

LEVEL	PASSWORD
2	Right, A, Right, B, Left, Down
3	Down, Right, B, Right, Down, B
4	Right, Right, Down, A, Down, A
5	Up, A, A, Down, Left, Up
6	Left, Up, A, B, B, Right
End	Down, Left, Up, A, Down, Right

A
B
C
D
E
F
G
H
I
J
K
L
M
N
O
P
Q
R
S
T
U
V
W
X
Y
Z

INSPECTOR GADGET

PASSWORDS

LEVEL	PASSWORD
2	FH2KBH
3	FM!PQM
4	FRVTLR
5	FWQZ!?

JEREMY MCGRATH SUPERCROSS 2000

250CC CLASS

Enter **SHJBBCGB** as a password.

THE JUNGLE BOOK: MOWGLI'S WILD ADVENTURE

LEVEL SELECT

Enter **BMHG** as a password.

CHEAT MODE

Press **SELECT** during a game to access the Options. Select Music/Effects and play the following in order:

40, 30, 20, 19, 18, 17, 16, 15.

KONAMI GAME BOY COLLECTION VOL. 1

LEVEL SELECT FOR CONTRA

At the Title Screen, enter **Up, Up, Down, Down, Left, Right, Left, Right, B, A, B, A, START**.

THE LEGEND OF ZELDA: ORACLE OF AGES

ITEMS LIST

BASIC ITEM	LOCATION/NECESSARY TASK	EFFECTS
Wooden Sword	Impa	Attack: 2
Noble Sword	Trading items quest by Return Linking	Attack: 3
Master Sword	Trading items quest while Main Linked by Return Linking	Attack: 5
Biggoron's Sword	Return Linking	Attack: 5
Wooden Shield	Sold at the Shop (30 Rupees)/Equipped when Main Linked	Regular Shield. Takes damage.
Iron Shield	Crescent Island Tokay Trader (Past) by Return Linking	Immune to more attacks than Wooden Shield
Mirror Shield	Crescent Island Tokay Trader (Past) while Main Linked by Return Linking	Best Shield. Immune to a lot more attacks and gets less damage
Ricky's Flute	Ricky while Main Linked	Ricky will come when the flute is played
Dimitri's Flute	Dimitri while Main Linked	Dimitri will come when the flute is played

A
B
C
D
E
F
G
H
I
J
K
L
M
N
O
P
Q
R
S
T
U
V
W
X
Y
Z

BASIC ITEM	LOCATION/NECESSARY TASK	EFFECTS
Moosh's Flute	Moosh in the Fairies Woods	Moosh will come when the flute is played
Strange Flute	Return Linking	No effect
Seed Satchel	Maku Tree (Present) after rescuing her	Can carry Seeds
Bombs	Ambi's Palace	Break cracked walls and blocks or attack enemies
Power Bracelet	Level 1 Dungeon	Can pick up a rock, sign, bush and vase when equipped
Roc's Feather	Level 2 Dungeon	Can jump one space. Can jump further when the Pegasus Seeds are used
Seed Shooter	Level 3 Dungeon	Can shoot Seeds in eight directions
Switch Hook	Level 4 Dungeon	Switches the location of the player and the target
Cane of Somaria	Level 5 Dungeon	Creates a block in front of the player
Mermaid Suit	Level 7 Dungeon	Needed to swim to deeper areas in the sea. Press the B Button to go to the seabed field and press the + Control Pad repeatedly to swim

BASIC ITEM	LOCATION/NECESSARY TASK	EFFECTS
Long Hook	Level 8 Dungeon	Quicker and loner in length than the Switch Hook
Shovel	Inside the Black Tower (Past)	Can dig the ground and remove the earth and sand
Boomerang	Target Carts mini-game a second time	Can turn on a distant switch and draw an item. Also, can stop an enemy from moving
Ember Seeds	Mystical tree in Labrynna	Can burn signs and bushes and light torches
Mystery Seeds	Mystical tree in Labrynna	Can get hints from the blue owl. Random effect when shot
Scent Seeds	Plant the Scent Seedling cm Crescent Island	Can attract certain monsters to the scent
Pegasus Seeds	Mystical tree in Labrynna	Can run faster and jump further. Also, can stop an enemy from moving
Gale Seeds	Mystical tree in Labrynna	Can warp the player to a mystical tree. Can blow away an enemy when shot
Harp of Ages	Nayru's house	Can play Tunes to warp time
Tune of Echoes	When receiving the Harp	Can give vitality to a dormant Time Hole
Tune of Currents	Tokkey in the lake of Talus Peaks	Can warp from the past to present

A B C D E F G H I J K **L** M N O P Q R S T U V W X Y Z

BASIC ITEM	LOCATION/NECESSARY TASK	EFFECTS
Tune of Ages	After rescuing Nayru in Ambi's Palace	Can warp freely throughout time
Zora's Flippers	Cheval's Grave	Can swim faster by pressing the A Button and dive by pressing the B Button
Magic Potion	Sold at Syrup's Shop/Can get from Maple event	Can revive the player when dead
Maku Seed	Maku Tree after collecting all 8 Essences	Break the spell of Onox's Castle
Gasha Seed	Scattered throughout the game in Dungeon chests and hidden locations	Varied effects
Magic Ring	Scattered throughout the game in Dungeon chests and hidden locations/ Get by growing a Gasha Seed/Can get from Maple event	Varied effects
Graveyard Key	Room behind the tomb at Yoll Graveyard	Needed to enter the Level 1 Dungeon
Cheval Rope	Cheval's Grave	Needed to make a raft
Island Chart	Tingle	Needed to sail on a raft

BASIC ITEM	LOCATION/NECESSARY TASK	EFFECTS
Scent Seedling	Mini-game on Crescent Island	Needed to get the Scent Seeds
Cracked Tuni Nut	Middle House in Symmetry City	Get this fixed to get the Tuni Nut
Tuni Nut	Get the Tuni Nut fixed by Patch	Needed to stop the volcano in Symmetry Village
Crown Key	Rescue the Goron Elder	Needed to enter the Level 5 Dungeon
Brotherhood Symbol	Goron's dancing mini-game (only when playing as 1st game)	Needed to get past the guard in front of the Goron Dance Hall
Rock Brisket	Target Carts mini game	Needed at the Goron Dance Hall in the Present
Lava Juice	Goron Shooting Gallery (Past)	Needed to get the Letter of Introduction
Goron Vase	Give the Rock Brisket to the guardian at the Goron Dance Hall (Present)	Needed at the Goron Dance Hall in the Past
Goronade	Give the Goron Vase to the guardian at the Goron Dance Hall (Past)	Needed to open the Bomb-dodging mini-game at the Big Bang
Letter of Introduction	Collect Old Mermaid Key and Lava Juice	Needed to get the Mermaid Key
Mermaid Key	Give the Letter of Introduction to Graceful Goron (Present), then beat him	Needed to enter the Level 6 Dungeon (Present)
Old Mermaid Key	Prize for the Bomb-dodging game at the Big Bang	Needed to enter the Level 6 Dungeon (Past)

A B C D E F G H I J K L M N O P Q R S T U V W X Y Z

BASIC ITEM	LOCATION/NECESSARY TASK	EFFECTS
Library Key	Rescue King Zora (Present) after rescuing King Zora (Past)	Needed to enter the Library
Book of Seals	Library of the Present	Needed to get the Fairy Powder at the Library in the past
Fairy Powder QueenZora Scale	Library in the Past Beat the Level 7 Dungeon	Needed to break the curse of the Fairy Needed to enter the Sea of Storms
Tokay Eyeball	Exchange with the Zora Scale Tablet for this with the Pirate Captain	Needed to enter Veran's Castle
Slate	Level 8 Dungeon	Four are needed to unlock the stairs to the Boss Key in the Level 8 Dungeon

THE LEGEND OF ZELDA: ORACLE OF SEASONS

ITEMS LIST

BASIC ITEM	LOCATION/NECESSARY TASK	EFFECTS
Wooden Sword	Hero's Cave/Already equipped when Main Linked	Attack: 2
Noble Sword	Lost Woods from trading items quest/ Get this by Return Linking	Attack: 3
Master Sword	Lost Woods from trading items quest while Main Linked/Get this by Return Linking	Attack: 5
Biggoron's Sword	Get this by Return Linking	Attack: 5
Wooden Shield	Sold at the Shop (30 Rupees)	Regular Shield. Takes damage.
Iron Shield	The blacksmith/Get this by Return Linking	Immune to more attacks than Wooden Shield
Mirror Shield	The blacksmith while Main Linked/Get this and gets less damage	Best Shield. Immune to a lot more attacks

A
B
C
D
E
F
G
H
I
J
K
L
M
N
O
P
Q
R
S
T
U
V
W
X
Y
Z

BASIC ITEM	LOCATION/NECESSARY TASK	EFFECTS
Ricky's Flute	Ricky if the player does not have other flute	Ricky will come when the flute is played
Wooden Shield	Sold at the Shop (30 Rupees)	Regular Shield. Takes damage.
Iron Shield	The blacksmith/Get this by Return Linking	Immune to more attacks than Wooden Shield
Mirror Shield	The blacksmith while Main Linked/Get this by Return Linking	Best Shield. Immune to a lot more attacks and gets less damage
Ricky's Flute	Ricky if the player does not have other flute	Ricky will come when the flute is played
Dimitri's Flute	Dimitri while Main Linked	Dimitri will come when the flute is played
Moosh's Flute	Moosh while Main Linked	Moosh will come when the flute is played
Strange Flute	Get this by Return Linking	No effect
Seed Satchel	Level 1 Dungeon	Can carry Seeds
Bombs	Level 2 Dungeon	Break cracked walls and blocks or attack enemies

BASIC ITEM	LOCATION/NECESSARY TASK	EFFECTS
Power Bracelet	Level 2 Dungeon	Can pick up a rock, sign, bush, and vase when equipped
Roc's Feather	Level 3 Dungeon	Can jump one space. Can jump further when the Pegasus Seeds are used
Slingshot	Level 4 Dungeon	Can shoot Seeds in eight directions
Magnetic Gloves	Level 5 Dungeon	Can move things by magnetic force. Useful when solving puzzles
Magical Boomerang	Level 6 Dungeon	Can control this with the + Control Pad while the button is pressed
Roc's Cape	Level 7 Dungeon	Can jump 3 spaces
Hyper Slingshot	Level 8 Dungeon	3-way slingshot
Shovel	Holly	Can dig the ground and remove the earth and sand
Boomerang	Subrosian dance mini-game	Can turn on a distant switch and draw an item. Also, can stop an enemy from moving
Fool's Ore	Roc's Feather Robbery Event	Can be used to attack
Ember Seeds	Mystical tree in Holodrum	Can burn signs and bushes and light torches

A
B
C
D
E
F
G
H
I
J
K
L
M
N
O
P
Q
R
S
T
U
V
W
X
Y
Z

BASIC ITEM	LOCATION/NECESSARY TASK	EFFECTS
Mystery Seeds	Mystical tree in Holodrum	Can get hints from the blue owl. Random effect when shot
Scent Seeds	Mystical tree in Holodrum	Can attract certain monsters to the scent
Pegasus Seeds	Mystical tree in Holodrum	Can run faster and jump further. Also, can stop an enemy from moving
Gale Seeds	Mystical tree in Holodrum	Can warp the player to a mystical tree. Can blow away an enemy when shot
Rod of Seasons	Temple of Seasons	Can change the seasons
Power of Spring	Temple of Seasons	Changes the season to Spring
Power of Summer	Summer Spirit	Changes the season to Summer
Power of Autumn	Autumn Spirit	Changes the season to Autumn
Power of Winter	Winter Spirit	Changes the season to Winter
Zora's Flippers	Complete the master diver's task	Can swim faster by pressing the A Button and dive by pressing the B Button
Magic Potion	Sold at Syrup's Shop/Can get from Maple event	Can revive the player when dead

BASIC ITEM	LOCATION/NECESSARY TASK	EFFECTS
Maku Seed	Maku Tree after collecting all 8 Essences	Break the spell of Onox's Castle
Gasha Seed	Scattered throughout the game in Dungeon chests and hidden locations	Varied effects
Magic Ring	Scattered throughout the game in Dungeon chests and hidden locations/ Get by growing a Gasha Seed/ Can get from Maple event	Varied effects
Ricky's Gloves	Beat Blaino	Needed to make Ricky a partner
Bomb Flower	Subrosia Village	Needed to enter the Tower of Autumn in the Temple of Seasons
Gnarled Key	Wake up the Maku Tree	Need to enter the Level 1 Dungeon
Floodgate Key	Floodgate Keeper's house	Needed to open the floodgate
Dragon Key	Mt. Cucco	Needed to enter the Level 4 Dungeon
Rusty Bell	Samasa Desert	Needed for the Pirate's Ship to leave
Pirate's Bell	Take the Rusty Bell to the blacksmith	Needed for the Pirate's Ship to leave
Master's Plaque	Complete the master diver's task to get this	Needed to get Zora's Flippers

BASIC ITEM	LOCATION/NECESSARY TASK	EFFECTS
Treasure Map	Sold at the basement shop in Horon Village	Needed to collect the Jewels
Member's Card	Sold at Subrosia Market	Needed to enter the hidden shop
Star-Shaped Ore	Dig up the ground at Subrosia seaside	Needed to get the Ribbon
Ribbon	Trade in the Star-Shaped Ore at Subrosia Market	Needed to go on a date with Rosa
Spring Banana	Mt. Cucco	Needed to make Moosh a partner
Jewels	Locations listed on the Treasure Map	Needed to enter Tarm Ruins
Red Ore	Subrosia Village	Needed to get the Hard Ore
Blue Ore	Subrosia Village	Needed to get the Hard Ore
Hard Ore	Take the Red and Blue Ore to the blast furnace	Needed to get the better Shield

LEGEND OF ZELDA: ORACLE OF SEASONS & AGES

RING INDEX

RING NUMBER	RING NAME	GAME VERSION	GASHA SEED OR MAPLE ENCOUNTER	LOCATION/ TASK	EFFECT 1=1/8 HEART
1	Friendship Ring	Both	No	Vasu's Ring Shop	None
2	Power Ring L-1	Seasons	No	Level 7 Dungeon	Attack +1 Damage +2
3	Power Ring L-2	Both	Yes		Attack +2 Damage +4
4	Power Ring L-3	Seasons	No	Second Hero's Cave	Attack +3 Damage +8
5	Armor Ring L-1	Ages	No		Attack -1 Damage -1
6	Armor Ring L-2	Seasons	No	Cave on Rolling Ridge	Attack -1 Damage -2
7	Armor Ring L-3	Ages	No	Second Hero's Cave	Attack -1 Damage -3
8	Red Ring	Seasons	No	Beat all 4 Golden Monsters in the Underground	Doubles the Attack
9	Blue Ring	Ages	No	Below a statue in Yoll Graveyard	Reduces Damage by 1/2
10	Green Ring	Both	Yes		Attack x 1.5 Damage x 0.75
11	Cursed Ring	Both	Yes		Attack x 0.5 Damage x 2
12	Expert's Ring	Both	Yes		A strong punch can be thrown when nothing is equipped
13	Blast Ring	Seasons	No		Power of the Bomb +2

A
B
C
D
E
F
G
H
I
J
K
L
M
N
O
P
Q
R
S
T
U
V
W
X
Y
Z

RING NUMBER	RING NAME	GAME VERSION	GASHA SEED OR MAPLE ENCOUNTER	LOCATION/ TASK	EFFECT 1=1/8 HEART
14	Rang Ring L-1	Seasons	No		Power of the Boomerang +1
15	Ages GBA Ring	Ages	No	Advance Shop	None
16	Maple's Ring	Both	Yes		Reduces the number of enemies needed to defeat by 1/2 in order to meet Maple
17	Steadfast Ring	Seasons	No	Level 8 Dungeon	Reduces the kickback by 1/2
18	Pegasus Ring	Ages	No		Pegasus Seed lasts twice as long
19	Toss Ring	Both	Yes	Bomb-dodging mini-game	Can throw object twice as far
20	Heart Ring L-1	Ages (Return Linking)	No	Fairy at the Temple of Seasons	Recovers lost Hearts as you walk
21	Heart Ring L-2	Both	Yes		Recovers lost Hearts
22	Swimmer's Ring	Ages (Return Linking)	No	Play mini-game in Sunken City after beating game	Swim faster
23	Charge Ring	Both	Yes		Spin Attack charges quickly (x4)
24	Light Ring L-1	Ages	No	Cave in Nuun Plateau	Shoot the Sword Beams at -2 Hearts
25	Light Ring L-2	Ages	No	Lynna Village mini-game	Shoot the Sword Beams at -3 Hearts
26	Bomber's Ring	Ages	No	Goron Dance mini-game	Set 2 Bombs at once

RING NUMBER	RING NAME	GAME VERSION	GASHA SEED OR MAPLE ENCOUNTER	LOCATION/TASK	EFFECT 1=$\frac{1}{8}$ HEART
27	Green Luck Ring	Both	No	Second Hide-and-Seek game (Ages)/Mayor Plen's house (Seasons)	Reduces damage from traps by 1/2
28	Blue Luck Ring	Both	Yes		Reduces damage from beams by 1/2
29	Yellow Luck Ring	Ages	No	Ambi's Palace	Reduces damage of falls by 1/2
30	Red Luck Ring	Both	Yes	Lynna Village mini-game	Reduces damage from spiked floors
31	Green Holy Ring	Both	Yes	Goron Dance mini-game	Reduces damage from electricity
32	Blue Holy Ring	Both	Yes	Lynna Village mini-game	No damage from Zora's fire
33	Red Holy Ring	Both	Yes	Second Subrosian Dance or Hide-and-Seek minigame (Seasons)/ Bottom of the ocean (Ages)	No damage from small rocks
34	Snowshoe Ring	Ages (Return Linking)	No	Mamamu Yan's mini-game	No sliding on ice
35	Roc's Ring	Both	Yes		Cracked floors don't crumble
36	Quicksand Ring	Both	Yes	Inside a cave (Seasons)/Bomb-Dodging mini-game (Ages)	No sinking in quicksand
37	Red Joy Ring	Both	Yes		Beasts drop double Rupees
38	Blue Joy Ring	Both (Main Linking)	No	After rescuing Princess Zelda	Beasts drop double Hearts
39	Yellow Joy Ring	Ages	No		Find double items

RING NUMBER	RING NAME	GAME VERSION	GASHA SEED OR MAPLE ENCOUNTER	LOCATION/TASK	EFFECT 1=1/8 HEART
40	Green Joy Ring	Seasons	No		Find double Ore Chunks
41	Discovery Ring	Both	No	Level 1 Dungeon	Sense soft earth nearby
42	Rang Ring L-2	Both	Yes		Power of the Boomerang +2
43	Octo Ring	Both	Yes	A cave (Seasons) / Lynna Village mini-game (Ages)	Become an Octorok
44	Moblin Ring	Both	Yes		Become a Moblin
45	Like Like Ring	Both	Yes	Level 7 Dungeon	Become a Like Like
46	Subrosian Ring	Seasons	No	Talon's cave	Become a Subrosian
47	First Gen Ring	Both	Yes		Become Link from the very first Zelda
48	Spin Ring	Seasons (Return Linking)	No	Talk to Mayor Plen	Double Spin Attack
49	Flower Ring	Both	Yes	Goron Dance Gold mini-game	No damage from own Bombs
50	Energy Ring	Both	Yes		Beam replaces Spin Attack
51	Dbl-Edged Ring	Both	Yes		Attack: 8 (consumes one Heart at a time)
52	Seasons GBA Ring	Seasons	No	Advance Shop	None
53	Slayer's Ring	Both	No	Vasu's Ring Shop	1000 beasts slain

RING NUMBER	RING NAME	GAME VERSION	GASHA SEED OR MAPLE ENCOUNTER	LOCATION/ TASK	EFFECT 1=⅛ HEART
54	Wealth Ring	Both	No	Vasu's Ring Shop	10,000 Rupees collected
55	Victory Ring	Both	No	Automatically obtain it when playing through the game a second time	Ganon is defeated
56	Sign Ring	Seasons	No	Break 100 signs then talk to a Subrosian	100 signs broken
57	100th Ring	Both	No	Vasu's Ring Shop	100 Rings appraised
58	Whisp Ring	Both	Yes		No effect from jinxes
59	Gasha Ring	Both	Yes		Grow great Gasha Seeds
60	Peace Ring	Both	Yes		No explosion while holding Bomb
61	Zora Ring	Both	Yes		Dive without breathing
62	Fist Ring	Both	Yes		Can throw punch when nothing is equipped
63	Whimsical Ring	Both	Yes		Attack becomes 1. Sometimes can beat an enemy with one hit (1 out of 256)
64	Protection Ring	Both	Yes		Damage taken is always 1 Heart

A
B
C
D
E
F
G
H
I
J
K
L
M
N
O
P
Q
R
S
T
U
V
W
X
Y
Z

LITTLE NICKY

A FAR BETTER PLACE

Enter **Evilray, Evilray, Innerlight, Possession** as a password.

LOONEY TUNES: TWOUBLE

PASSWORDS

Granny's House Pt.1: Dog, Granny, Tweety, Taz, Sylvester

Granny's Cellar Pt.1: Taz, Sylvester, Tweety, Dog, Granny

Garden Pt.1: Sylvester, Tweety, Dog, Taz, Granny

Out in the Streets Pt.1: Dog, Tweety, Taz, Granny, Sylvester

ToyShop Pt.1: Taz, Dog, Tweety, Sylvester, Granny

M&M'S MINIS MADNESS

PASSWORDS

LEVEL	PASSWORD
1-2	Yellow, Red, Blue, Blue, Green, Blue
1-3	Green, Blue, Yellow, Red, Yellow, Yellow
2-1	Green, Blue, Green, Red, Green, Yellow
2-2	Red, Yellow, Orange, Yellow, Brown, Blue
2-3	Brown, Green, Red, Blue, Orange, Blue

MEN IN BLACK: THE SERIES 2

PASSWORDS

LEVEL	PASSWORD
2	MTTH
3	STVN
4	SPDM
5	BTHH
6	BBYH
7	MRLL
8	MMDD

METAL GEAR SOLID

NEW OBJECTIVES

Complete the game on EASY to unlock new objectives for the original levels.

UNLOCK SOUND MODE

Beat all the VR missions: Time Attack and Practice Mode.

MOON PATROL/SPY HUNTER

INFINITE LIVES IN MOON PATROL

At the title screen, press **Up, Down, Left, Right, Up, Down, Left, Right, Up, Left, Down, A.**

ALL SPECIAL WEAPONS IN SPY HUNTER

At the title screen, press **Up, Down, Left, Right, Up, Down, Left, Right, Up, Left, Down, B.**

MR. NUTZ

LEVEL PASSWORDS

LEVEL	PASSWORD
2	DDMMNN
3	NNRRGG
4	CCLLRS
5	JJMPPR
6	SWWTCH

Level 6

NASCAR RACERS

PASSWORDS

TRACK	PASSWORD
Jungle 2	KTHZTRYW
Jungle 3	PXMMZCHW
Jungle 4	TYGNDPTS
Egypt 1	LYMTHXRS
Egypt 2	ZTCSMGZW
Egypt 3	DYCLNSDR
Egypt 4	DTDWWYDZ

TRACK	PASSWORD
Europe 1	CNCMCCML
Europe 2	DSTZLCTY
Europe 3	NHKMZRXZ
Europe 4	LSCLLLZS
St. Petersburg 1	LTNTHHCX
St. Petersburg 2	WHXSSTNT
St. Petersburg 3	NYLWNDSW
St. Petersburg 4	PGPMWKPY

A
B
C
D
E
F
G
H
I
J
K
L
M
N
O
P
Q
R
S
T
U
V
W
X
Y
Z

NBA JAM TOURNAMENT EDITION

NO PENALTY FOR GOAL TENDING

On the "Tonight's Match Up" screen, press **Right, Up, Down, Right, Down, Up.**

EASIER INTERCEPTIONS

On the "Tonight's Match Up" screen, press **Left, Left, Left, Left, A, Right.**

EASIER THREE-POINTERS

On the "Tonight's Match Up" screen, press **Up, Down, Left, Right, Left, Down, Up.**

SLIPPERY COURT

On the "Tonight's Match Up" screen, press **A, A, A, A, A, Right, Right, Right, Right, Right.**

HIGH SHOTS

On the "Tonight's Match Up" screen, press **Up, Down, Up, Down, Right, Up, A, A, A, A, Down.**

DISPLAY SHOT PERCENTAGE

On the "Tonight's Match Up" screen, press **Up, Up, Down, Down, B.**

CONTINUED

SUPER DUNKS

On the "Tonight's Match Up" screen, press **Left, Right, A, B, B, A.**

ALWAYS ON FIRE

On the "Tonight's Match Up" screen, press **Down, Right, Right, B, A, Left.**

NEW ADVENTURES OF MARY KATE AND ASHLEY

LEVEL PASSWORDS

LEVEL	PASSWORD
Volcano Mystery	CBTHPM
Haunted Camp	GMQTCK
Funhouse Mystery	LHDDQJ
Hotel Who-Done-It	MDGKMQ

ODDWORLD INHABITANTS

LEVEL	PASSWORD
2-0	JCBCM
2-1	JMBCC
2-2	JMCCB
2-3	JPCCD
2-4	JTCCJ
2-5	STCCS
2-6	SBCCT
2-7	TBFCQ
3-1	TBKCL
3-2	TBTCB
3-3	TBTDC
3-4	TBTGF
End	TBTBT

PAC MAN: SPECIAL COLOR EDITION

PASSWORDS

STAGE	PASSWORD
Stage 1:	STR
Stage 2:	HNM
Stage 3:	KST
Stage 4:	TRT
Stage 5:	MYX
Stage 6:	KHL
Stage 7:	RTS
Stage 8:	SKB
Stage 9:	HNT
Stage 10:	SRY
Stage 11:	YSK
Stage 12:	RCF
Stage 13:	HSM
Stage 14:	PWW
Stage 15:	MTN
Stage 16:	TKY
Stage 17:	RGH
Stage 18:	TNS
Stage 19:	YKM
Stage 20:	MWS
Stage 21:	KTY
Stage 22:	TYK
Stage 23:	SMM
Stage 24:	NFL
Stage 25:	SRT
Stage 26:	KKT
Stage 27:	MDD
Stage 28:	CWD
Stage 29:	DRC

A
B
C
D
E
F
G
H
I
J
K
L
M
N
O
P
Q
R
S
T
U
V
W
X
Y
Z

CONTINUED

STAGE	PASSWORD
Stage 30:	WHT
Stage 31:	FLT
Stage 32:	SKM
Stage 33:	QTN
Stage 34:	SMN
Stage 39:	THD
Stage 40:	RMN
Stage 41:	CNK
Stage 42:	FRB
Stage 43:	MLR
Stage 44:	FRP
Stage 45:	SDB
Stage 46:	BQJ
Stage 47:	VSM
Stage 48:	RDY
Stage 49:	XLP
Stage 50:	WLC
Stage 51:	TMF
Stage 52:	QNS
Stage 53:	GWR
Stage 54:	PLT
Stage 55:	KRW
Stage 56:	HRC
Stage 57:	RPN
Stage 58:	CNT
Stage 59:	BTT
Stage 60:	TMR
Stage 61:	MNS
Stage 62:	SWD
Stage 63:	LDM
Stage 86:	DCR
Stage 97:	PNN

PERFECT DARK

UNLOCK CHEATS IN N64 VERSION

Use your Game Boy version of Perfect Dark to unlock four cheats on your N64 version of Perfect Dark. Use a Transfer Pak and download your information from the Game Boy version to the N64 version. This will make four cheats available. You'll now have the Cloaking Device, Hurricane Fists, the R-Tracker, and every gun in Solo Mode on the N64 version of Perfect Dark!

POWERPUFF GIRLS: BAD MOJO JOJO

BUTTERCUP GRAPHIC

Enter **CHEMICALX** at the Enter Secrets screen.

BUBBLES GRAPHIC

Enter **BOOGIEMAN** at the Enter Secrets screen.

MAYOR GRAPHIC

Enter **BROCCOLOID** at the Enter Secrets screen.

BOOMER GRAPHIC

Enter **USESNIPS** at the Enter Secrets screen.

BUTCH GRAPHICS

Enter **BESNAILS** at the Enter Secrets screen.

BRICK GRAPHICS

Enter **TAILSRULE** at the Enter Secrets screen.

CONTINUED

UNLIMITED LIVES
Enter **DOGMODE** at the Enter Secrets screen.

UNLIMITED RED CHEMICALX
Enter **CHERRY** at the Enter Secrets screen.

UNLIMITED BLACK CHEMICALX
Enter **LICORICE** at the Enter Secrets screen.

UNLIMITED FLIGHT
Enter **IGOTWINGS** at the Enter Secrets screen.

MESSAGE AND PHOTO
Enter **BILLSGIRLS** at the Enter Secrets screen.

ANOTHER MESSAGE AND PHOTO
Enter **RICHARDKIM** at the Enter Secrets screen.

POKEY OAKS SCHOOL LEVEL
Enter **GOGETBUTCH** at the Enter Secrets screen.

ART MUSEUM LEVEL
Enter **DUST BOOMER** at the Enter Secrets screen.

BRICK TRADING CARD
Enter **BESTBUYPWR** or **ZORCH** at the Enter Secrets screen.

PRINCESS TRADING CARD
Enter **SEARS** or **FIZZAT** at the Enter Secrets screen.

POWERPUFF GIRLS TRADING CARD
Enter **CITYRULES** or **TOYSTOWN** at the Enter Secrets screen.

PROFESSOR UTONIUM TRADING CARD
Enter **ANUBISHEAD** or **TARGETGAME** at the Enter Secrets screen.

ROACH COACH TRADING CARD
Enter **ROACHCOACH** at the Enter Secrets screen.

ROWDYRUFF BOYS TRADING CARD
Enter **DOGGIEDO** or **EBWORLD** at the Enter Secrets screen.

SARA BELLUM TRADING CARD
Enter **GAMESTOP** or **SNOWPOKE** at the Enter Secrets screen.

SEDUSA TRADING CARD
Enter **SEDUSA** at the Enter Secrets screen.

UTONIUM CHATEAU TRADING CARD
Enter **TOWNSVILLE** at the Enter Secrets screen.

VOLCANO MOUNTAIN TRADING CARD
Enter **TOYSRUSCOM** at the Enter Secrets screen.

A
B
C
D
E
F
G
H
I
J
K
L
M
N
O
P
Q
R
S
T
U
V
W
X
Y
Z

POWERPUFF GIRLS: BATTLE HIM

UNLIMITED RED CHEMICAL X

Enter **CANDYAPPLE** at the Enter Secrets screen.

UNLIMITED BLACK CHEMICAL X

Enter **MIDNIGHT** at the Enter Secrets screen.

UNLIMITED FLIGHT

Enter **JETFUEL** at the Enter Secrets screen.

UNLIMITED LIVES

Enter **UNDEAD** at the Enter Secrets screen.

UNLIMITED SUPER ATTACK

Enter **PHONECARD** at the Enter Secrets screen.

BLOSSOM GRAPHIC

Enter **MISSKEANE** at the Enter Secrets screen.

BUTTERCUP GRAPHIC

Enter **LUMPKINS** at the Enter Secrets screen.

BOOMER GRAPHIC

Enter **WANTSNIPS** at the Enter Secrets screen.

BUTCH GRAPHIC

Enter **SNAILSIAM** at the Enter Secrets screen.

BRICK GRAPHIC

Enter **ITOOKTAILS** at the Enter Secrets screen.

MAYOR GRAPHIC

Enter **MCCRACKEN** at the Enter Secrets screen.

TOWNSVILLE SKIES LEVEL

Enter **GOGETBUTCH** at the Enter Secrets screen.

UTONIUM CHATEAU LEVEL

Enter **BEATBRICK** at the Enter Secrets screen.

MESSAGE AND PHOTO

Enter **BILLSGIRLS** at the Enter Secrets screen.

ANOTHER MESSAGE AND PHOTO

Enter **RICHARDKIM** at the Enter Secrets screen.

ART MUSEUM CARD

Enter **MALPHS** at the Enter Secrets screen.

BOOGIEMAN CARD

Enter **HOTLINE** or **ELBO** at the Enter Secrets screen.

BOOMER CARD

Enter **ICEBREATH** or **BESTBUYHDQ** at the Enter Secrets screen.

CITY OF TOWNSVILLE CARD

Enter **TOYSPOWER** or **TALKINGDOG** at the Enter Secrets screen.

EVIL CAT CARD

Enter **POWERPUFF** at the Enter Secrets screen.

CONTINUED

MAYOR CARD

Enter **TOYSTOUGH** or **TARGETPUFF** at the Enter Secrets screen.

RAINBOW THE CLOWN CARD

Enter **MRSBELLUM** or **RICHMONDVA** at the Enter Secrets screen.

TALKING DOG CARD

Enter **BIGBILLY** or **RUFFBOYS** at the Enter Secrets screen.

TOWNSVILLE ART MUSEUM CARD

Enter **MALPHS** at the Enter Secrets screen.

TOWNSVILLE CITY HALL CARD

Enter **PRINCESS** at the Enter Secrets screen.

UTONIUM FAMILY CARD

Enter **FLEETFEET** or **GOTOSEARS** at the Enter Secrets screen.

POWERPUFF GIRLS: PAINT THE TOWNSVILLE GREEN

UNLIMITED RED CHEMICAL X

Enter **RUBIES** at the Enter Secrets screen.

UNLIMITED BLACK CHEMICAL X

Enter **EBONY** at the Enter Secrets screen.

UNLIMITED FLIGHT

Enter **IFLYINSKY** at the Enter Secrets screen.

UNLIMITED LIVES

Enter **QUICKENED** at the Enter Secrets screen.

UNLIMITED SUPER ATTACK

Enter **POWERCALL** at the Enter Secrets screen.

BLOSSOM GRAPHIC

Enter **POKEYOAKS** at the Enter Secrets screen.

BOOMER GRAPHIC

Enter **SNIPSFORME** at the Enter Secrets screen.

BUBBLES GRAPHIC

Enter **UTONIUM** at the Enter Secrets screen.

BUTCH GRAPHIC

Enter **LIKESNAILS** at the Enter Secrets screen.

BRICK GRAPHIC

Enter **GOTMETAILS** at the Enter Secrets screen.

MAYOR GRAPHIC

Enter **OCTIEVIL** at the Enter Secrets screen.

MESSAGE AND PHOTO

Enter **BILLSGIRLS** at the Enter Secrets screen.

ANOTHER MESSAGE AND PHOTO

Enter **RICHARDKIM** at the Enter Secrets screen.

BONSAI GARDEN LEVEL

Enter **DUSTBOOMER** at the Enter Secrets screen.

CONTINUED

UTONIUM CHATEAU LEVEL

Enter **BEATBRICK** at the Enter Secrets screen.

ACE CARD

Enter **WUNK** or **GOCIRCUIT** at the Enter Secrets screen.

BIG BILLY CARD

Enter **KABOOM** or **EBSTORE** at the Enter Secrets screen.

BROCCLOID EMPEROR CARD

Enter **MOJOJOJO** at the Enter Secrets screen.

BUTCH CARD

Enter **ROWDYRUFFS** at the Enter Secrets screen.

FUZZY LUMPKINS CARD

Enter **RZONE** at the Enter Secrets screen.

GRUBBER CARD

Enter **TOYSMAGIC** or **GRUBBER** at the Enter Secrets screen.

LITTLE ARTURO CARD

Enter **TOYSCIENCE** or **TARGETPOWR** at the Enter Secrets screen.

MS. KEANE CARD

Enter **FLEETFEET** or **SEARSRULES** at the Enter Secrets screen.

SNAKE CARD

Enter **SQUID** or **BESTBUYPUF** at the Enter Secrets screen.

TOWNSVILLE DUMP CARD

Enter **AMOEBABOYS** at the Enter Secrets screen.

ALL CARDS AND CHEATS

Enter **BILLHUDSON** at the Enter Secrets screen.

PUZZLE MASTER

PASSWORDS

LEVEL	PASSWORD
1	KING
2	FAIRY
3	WIZARD
4	MOUSE or CHAMPION

NOTE: Enter the word **CHEAT** as a password to have all of the tools right away.

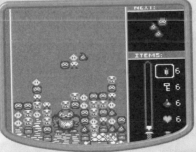

Level 4

PUZZLED

LEVEL SELECT

At the Password Screen, enter passwords **EL001** through **EL150**, where the number in the code chooses a level between 1 and 150.

RAYMAN

ALL LEVELS PASSWORD

Enter **CH5G4mSljD** as a password.

ACCESS ALL LEVELS

Pause the game and press **A, Left, A, Left, A, B, Right, B, Up, B, A, Left, A, Down, A.**

Access All Levels

FILL ENERGY

Pause the game and press **B, right, A, Up, B, Left, A, Down, B, Right.**

99 LIVES

Pause the game and press **A, Right, B, Up, A, Left, B, Down, A, Right, B, Up, A, Left, B.**

99 Lives

REVELATIONS: THE DEMON SLAYER

GET LOKI, PAZUZU, AND ASURA

Combine the following:

Suzaku + Kali = Asura (Asura has 1800 hp)
Zenon + Shiva = Pazuzu (Pazuzu has 1720 hp)
Zenon + Jinn = Loki (Loki has 1700 hp)

GET BAAL TO JOIN YOUR TEAM

First beat the game, then play the game again. This time return to Mt. Palo and talk to him. He'll join your team.

GET LUCIFER TO JOIN YOUR TEAM

First beat the game, then play it again; this time, return to the Cave of Oasis. Talk to him and he will join you and your team.

A SECRET CAVE

In Luciferium, walk to the northwest corner. Find the hidden cave by exploring the mountainous region. In the Cave you'll find the Omega Armor, Omega Sword, the Alpha Mail, and the Alpha Sword.

GET VAERIAL TO JOIN YOUR TEAM

First Beat the Game, then return to the Nest of Zord. Talk to the monster located on the former battleground.

CONTINUED

ITEM COMBINATIONS

Lich + Harpy = Kelpie	L15
Mammoth + Kobold = Blue	L12
Blue + Kobold = Kelpie	L15
Kobold + Tanki = Kimalis	L8
Kobold + Kelpie = Larun	L13
Mammoth + Hecket = Kelpie	L15
Blue + Kelpie = Kelpie	L15
Mammoth + Hecket = Gayle	L10
Blue + Hecket = Lich	L1

ROAD CHAMPS BXS STUNT BIKING

ALL MODES

Enter **QGF7** as a password.

RUGRATS IN PARIS - THE MOVIE

PASSWORDS

LEVEL	PASSWORD
2	QPRCHJNY
4	ZKHMRTBS

SABRINA THE ANIMATED SERIES: ZAPPED!

PASSWORDS

LEVEL	PASSWORD
1-2	Sabrina, Sabrina, Salem, Jem
1-3	Sabrina, Salem, Salem, Red Head Boy
1-4	Sabrina, Harvey, Salem, Harvey
2-1	Salem, Cloey, Sabrina, Salem
2-2	Harvey, Salem, Red Head Boy, Red Head Boy
2-3	Harvey, Harvey, Red Head Boy, Sabrina
2-4	Harvey, Cloey, Red Head Boy, Salem
3-1	Cloey, Jem, Jem, Harvey
3-2	Jem, Harvey, Cloey, Sabrina
3-3	Jem, Cloey, Cloey, Salem
3-4	Jem, Jem, Cloey, Salem
4-1	Red Head Boy, Red Head Boy, Harvey, Cloey
4-2	Sabrina, Cloey, Jem, Salem
4-3	Sabrina, Jem, Jem, Harvey
4-4	Sabrina, Red Head Boy, Jem, Cloey

A
B
C
D
E
F
G
H
I
J
K
L
M
N
O
P
Q
R
S
T
U
V
W
X
Y
Z

SAN FRANCISCO RUSH 2049

PASSWORDS

TRACK	PASSWORDS
2	MADTOWN
3	FATCITY
4	SFRISCO
5	GASWRKZ
6	SKYWAYZ
7	INDSTRL
8	NEOCHGO
9	RIPTIDE

Level 9

SCOOBY-DOO!
CLASSIC CREEP CAPERS

PASSWORDS

Select **CONTINUE** from the main menu and enter the following passwords:

Chapter One: It's A Mystery!

Chapter Two: Boo's Clues!

Chapter Three: Chemo-Sabotage!

CONTINUED

Chapter Four: Jailbreak!

Chapter Five: The Plan!

Chapter Six: Finale!

SHAMUS

PASSWORDS

LEVEL	PASSWORD
1	5GF3SGV1V
2	4GF3SGV1T
3	7GF3SGV1X
4	6GF3SGV1V

SHREK: FAIRY TALE FREAKDOWN

PASSWORDS

STAGE	PASSWORD
Village as Thelonius	LRSVGTLXM
Dungeon as Thelonius	YFSVGTLXK
Village as Shrek	SMHTVKCQR
Dungeon as Shrek	TQDFNHGGM
Swamp as Shrek	TFGKWLSJJ
Dark Forest as Shrek	KDNBQGKVY
Bridge as Shrek	KWJPYXCQC
Castle as Shrek	YNNHLBMBY

THE SIMPSONS: TREEHOUSE OF TERROR

PASSWORDS

LEVEL	PASSWORD
2	FWXCKJXGLWN
3	TNSLRYSJGWW
4	BXPGCFPYJWB
5	WSQJLTQFYWK
6	NPKYGBKTFWQ
7	XQRFJWRBTWP

A B C D E F G H I J K L M N O P Q R S T U V W X Y Z

SNOOPY TENNIS

SECRET CHARACTERS

Enter **WWXR** as a password.

SPAWN

NORMAL DIFFICULTY PASSWORDS

LEVEL	PASSWORD
2	Heart, Heart, Skull, Heart
3	Heart, Skull, Skull, Blank
4	Skull, Spawn, Skull, Heart
5	Heart, Skull, Spawn, Spawn
6	Spawn, Spawn, Heart, Blank
7	Skull, Spawn, Spawn, Heart

HARD DIFFICULTY PASSWORDS

LEVEL	PASSWORD
2	Blank, Heart, Spawn, Heart
3	Spawn, Skull, Blank, Skull
4	Heart, Spawn, Skull, Spawn
5	Spawn, Heart, Blank, Spawn
6	Skull, Skull, Spawn, Heart
7	Spawn, Heart, Skull, Spawn

SPIDER-MAN

PASSWORDS

GAME LOCATION	PASSWORD
Venom defeated	GVCBF
Lizard defeated	QVCLF
Lab	G-FGN

Lab Level

SPIDER-MAN 2: THE SINISTER SIX

EASY PASSWORDS

LEVEL	PASSWORD
Pier	QQ1M9G
World Trade Center	NP2G7F
Madison Square Garden	QKPO9J
Central Park	MMPT1D
Empire State University Labs	48919Z

A
B
C
D
E
F
G
H
I
J
K
L
M
N
O
P
Q
R
S
T
U
V
W
X
Y
Z

MEDIUM PASSWORDS

LEVEL	PASSWORD
Pier	33M8P!
World Trade Center	!LQM92
Madison Square Garden	SF679G
Central Park	3DJ!R8
Empire State University Labs	QC6F1B

HARD PASSWORDS

LEVEL	PASSWORD
Pier	RCXM!H
World Trade Center	PJ1N1D
Madison Square Garden	Z8CFRO
Central Park	X9N435
Empire State University Labs	Q63F1B

SPONGEBOB SQUAREPANTS: LEGEND OF THE LOST SPATULA

LEVEL SELECT AND ALL ITEMS

Select **CONTINUE** and enter **D3BVG-M0D3**. When you pause the game, you should see a Level Select option.

STAR WARS: EPISODE 1 RACER

A FASTER ANAKIN

Collect every racer and Anakin will go 735 mph.

TURBO START

Press the throttle button as the 1 fades.

STAR WARS: EPISODE 1 OBI-WAN'S ADVENTURES

PASSWORDS

LEVEL	PASSWORD
2	BQVQK
3	WNLRM
4	SDGNK
5	CNLML
6	BXGTG
7	QSRVJ
8	TKGJZ
9	LPZCP

Level 9
The Final Battle
Password: LPZCP

SUPER MARIO BROS. DX

YOU VS. BOO RACE LEVELS

Get 100,000 points in one "normal" game to access these head-to-head stages.

UNLOCK SMB FOR SUPER PLAYERS

Get 300,000 points in one "normal" game to unlock Super Mario Bros. for Super Players. This is the same as the Japanese SMB 2/Super Mario: The Lost Levels, except that Luigi is not available. Instead, Mario has Luigi's higher jumping abilities.

CONTINUED

LEVEL SELECT

When you beat the game once, you can select your starting point.

YOSHI EGG FINDER IN CHALLENGE MODE

Once you've found at least one Yoshi Egg, a Yoshi option should appear in the Toy Box. Select it, and a random level's Egg location will be shown. At first, it only shows the screen you should find the egg on, but as you get more eggs, the hints become more detailed.

ALBUM PICTURES

To get all the album pictures, do the following:

Page 1:	(Top-Left) Fill up the Score Meter in Challenge
	(Top-Right) Get every medal in Challenge
	(Middle) Beat Original Mode
	(Bottom-Left) Beat all the Star Levels in Original
	(Bottom Right) Beat SMB for Super Players
Page 2:	(Top-Left) Get the end-of-level Fireworks
	(Top-Middle) Get a 1-Up Mushroom
	(Top-Right) Find and climb a Bonus Stage Vine
	(Middle-Left) Beat Original 1985 Mode
	(Middle) Save the Princess
	(Middle-Right) Use the link cable to trade High Scores

	(Bottom-Left) Get every Red Coin medal in Challenge	A
	(Bottom-Middle) Get every High Score medal in Challenge	B
		C
	(Bottom-Right) Get every Yoshi Egg in Challenge	D
Page 3:	(Top-Left) Defeat a Little Goomba	E
	(Top-Middle) Defeat a Bloober	F
	(Top-Right) Defeat Lakitu	G
	(Middle-Left) Defeat a Cheep Cheep	H
	(Middle) Defeat a Hammer Brother	I
	(Middle-Right) Defeat a Bullet Bill	J
	(Bottom-Left) Defeat a Koopa Troopa	K
	(Bottom-Middle) Defeat a Spiny	L
	(Bottom-Right) Defeat a Buzzy Beetle	M
Page 4:	(Top-Left) Defeat Bowser in World 1 with fireballs	N
	(Top-Right) Defeat Bowser in World 2 with fireballs	O
	(Bottom-Left) Defeat Bowser in World 3 with fireballs	P
	(Bottom-Right) Defeat Bowser in World 4 with fireballs	Q
Page 5:	(Top-Left) Defeat Bowser in World 5 with fireballs	R
	(Top-Right) Defeat Bowser in World 6 with fireballs	S
	(Bottom-Left) Defeat Bowser in World 7 with fireballs	T
	(Bottom-Right) Defeat Bowser in World 8 with fireballs	U
		V
		W
		X
		Y
		Z

SURVIVAL KIDS

MINI GAMES

Fishing Game: Grab the big rock near the main river. Use the rock where you see fish.

Big Berry Game: First, get a monkey, then go to the big berry tree after the river. Use the monkey to play the game.

Egg Catcher Game: Go to the north end of the desert with the monkey.

TAZMANIAN DEVIL: MUNCHING MADNESS

LEVEL	PASSWORDS
BLGNGJPDFFTJ	Unlocks China Level
LMBPBKTFKDPK	Unlocks Switzerland Level

TEST DRIVE 6

UNLOCK CARS

Win the Mega Cup and unlock: **BMW V12 LMR**

PANOZ ROADSTER

You can select them at the "purchase car" screen.

UNLOCK THE MEGA CUP

Win all of the other tournaments to unlock the Mega Cup.

TONY HAWK'S PRO SKATER 2

ALL BOARDS AND LEVELS OPEN

Enter **B58LPTGBBBBV** as a password.

TOONSYLVANIA

PASSWORDS

LEVEL	PASSWORD
3	4F627
4	XVJRL
5	NMVN3

TUROK 3: SHADOW OF OBLIVION

UNLIMITED AMMUNITION

Enter **ZXLCPMZ** at the Password Screen.

Unlimited Ammo

UNLIMITED LIVES

Enter **FJVHDCK** at the Password Screen.

CONTINUED

SKIP LEVEL

Enter **XCDSDFS** at the Password Screen.

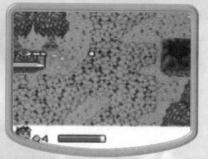

Level Skip

EASY PASSWORDS

LEVEL	PASSWORD
2	SDFLMSF
3	DVLFDZM
4	VFDSGPD
5	CSDJKFD

MEDIUM PASSWORDS

LEVEL	PASSWORD
2	VLXCZVF
3	DPSDCVX
4	ZMGFSCM
5	HWKLFYS

HARD PASSWORDS

LEVEL	PASSWORD
2	CJSDPSF
3	CMSDKCD
4	SPFPWLD
5	TPDFQGB

ULTIMATE PAINTBALL

PASSWORDS

LEVEL	PASSWORD
2	9GSMJY2K
3	16FWJJET
4	1B5WJWTO
5	13OWJBOY
6	CXXWJROB
7	C3SWJXIA
8	665WJQIU
9	9ZOCJTAK

WACKY RACES

ALL DRIVERS AND TRACKS

Enter **MUTTLEY** as a password.

All Drivers and Tracks

WORMS: ARMAGEDDON

LEVEL	PASSWORDS
Jungle	Pink worm, Banana bomb, Skeletal worm, Pink worm
Cheese	Pink worm, Banana bomb, Blue worm, Dynamite
Medical	Skeletal worm, Blue worm, Banana bomb, Banana bomb
Desert	Red worm, Pink worm, Skeletal worm, Blue worm
Tools	Banana bomb, Pink worm, Pink worm, Blue worm
Egypt	Skeletal worm, Pink worm, Red worm, Banana worm
Hell	Pink worm, Blue worm, Red worm, Dynamite
Tree-hut	Red worm, Skeletal worm, Dynamite, Blue worm
Garden	Banana bomb, Red worm, Skeletal worm, Dynamite
Snow	Dynamite, Pink worm, Blue worm, Blue worm
Constyrd	Pink worm, Pink worm, Banana bomb, Banana bomb
Pirate	Dynamite, Blue worm, Dynamite, Skeletal worm
Fruit	Skeletal worm, Red worm, Banana bomb, Skeletal worm
Alien	Dynamite, Blue worm, Red worm, Red worm
Circuit	Red worm, Dynamite, Dynamite, Dynamite
Medieval	Blue worm, Dynamite, Skeletal worm, Blue worm

X-MEN: MUTANT ACADEMY

APOCALYPSE

Press **Right, Left, Up, Down, Left, Up, B + A** at the title screen.

PHOENIX

Press **Down, Right, Down, Up, Left, Right, B + A** at the title screen.

X-MEN: MUTANT WARS

PASSWORDS

LEVEL	PASSWORD
2	0KNG6HWB
3	0LNG6HXQ
4	0LNF7HYP
5	0KPF7HZG
6	1KPF7H0D
7	1KPG7H19
8	1KPF7J2C
9	1KPF7J3L

X-MEN: WOLVERINE'S RAGE

LEVEL PASSWORDS

LEVEL	PASSWORD
2	Wolvie's Mask, Wolvie's Claws, X-Men Insignia, Wolvie's Torso
3	Wolvie's Claws, Sabertooth, Wolvie's Torso, Wolvie's Mask
4	Skull, Wolvie's Mask, X-Men Insignia, Wolvie's Claws
5	Cyber, Lady Deathstrike, Wolvie's Torso, X-Men Insignia
6	Wolvie's Mask, Wolvie's Torso, Wolvie's Head, Lady Deathstrike
7	Wolvie's Claws, Cyber, X-Men Insignia, Skull
8	Skull, X-Men Insignia, Wolvie's Claws, Sabertooth
End	Cyber, Skull, X-Men Insignia, Lady Deathstrike

ALTERNATE COSTUME

At the title screen, press **Up, Up, Down, Down, Left, Right, Left, Right, B, A.** You'll here Wolverine say, "All Right!"

XTREME SPORTS

CHEAT MENU

At the main menu, press **Left(5), Up(5), Right(5), Down(5), Select(5)**.

VIEW CREDITS

Enter your name as **"staff"** at the Sign-In. Exit the Sign-In and enter the Snack Hut to view the credits.

ALL COMPETITION MEDALS

Enter your name as **"xyzzy"** at the Sign-In. Exit the Sign–In, hold the **A Button** and press **SELECT**. Hold the **A Button** and press **SELECT** again to change the Medal count back to zero.

YARS' REVENGE

ALL LEVELS PASSWORD

Enter **Square, +, Square, Square** as a password. This will take you to Level 240.

A
B
C
D
E
F
G
H
I
J
K
L
M
N
O
P
Q
R
S
T
U
V
W
X
Y
Z

THE GAMES

GAME BOY® ADVANCE LEGEND

ABBREV.	WHAT IT MEANS
Left	Left on + Control Pad
Right	Right on + Control Pad
Up	Up on + Control Pad
Down	Down on + Control Pad
START	Press START
SELECT	Press SELECT
A	Press A Button
B	Press B Button
L	Left Shoulder Button
R	Right Shoulder Button

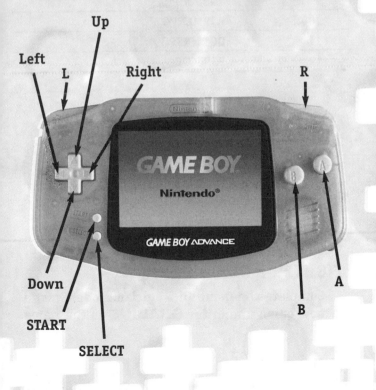

ARMY MEN ADVANCE

LEVEL SELECT

Enter **NQRDGTPB** as a password.

PASSWORDS

LEVEL	PASSWORD
2	HJRDCHMC
3	GGRSGJMC
4	FSRSMKMC
5	DQRNBBMC
6	CSRJGCMC
7	BQRDMDPC
8	TJRDQFPC
9	SGRSCQPC
10	RJRNLRPC
11	QGRNRSPC
12	PSRJCTPC

CASTLEVANIA: CIRCLE OF THE MOON

MAGICIAN MODE

Complete the game. Start a new game and enter **FIREBALL** as the name.

FIGHTER MODE

Complete the game in Magician mode. Start a new game and enter **GRADIUS** as the name.

SHOOTER MODE

Complete the game in Fighter mode. Start a new game and enter **CROSSBOW** as the name.

THIEF MODE

Complete the game in Shooter mode. Start a new game and enter **DAGGER** as the name.

CHU CHU ROCKET

HARD MODE

Complete Normal Mode to get Hard Mode.

SPECIAL MODE

Complete Hard Mode to get Special Mode.

MANIA MODE

Complete Special Mode to get Mania Mode.

EARTHWORM JIM

LEVEL SELECT

Pause the game and press **Right, R, B, A, L, L, A, R.**

LEVEL CODES

Pause the game and enter the following to skip to that level:

LEVEL	CODE
Buttville	L, A, Up, R, A, R, A, SELECT
Down the Tubes	Up, L, Down, A, R, A
For Pete's Sake	R, L, R, L, A, R
Level 5	R, L, A, B, B, A, L, R
Snot a Problem	R, Up, SELECT, L, R, Left
What the Heck	SELECT, R, B, Down, L, B

F-ZERO: MAXIMUM VELOCITY

SLY JOKER

Defeat Pawn, Knight, and Bishop on Standard difficulty.

THE STINGRAY

Defeat Pawn, Knight, and Bishop on Expert difficulty. This also opens the Queen series.

SILVER THUNDER

Defeat the Queen Series.

FALCON MK-II

Defeat the Pawn, Knight, Bishop, and Queen series on Expert difficulty.

MASTER DIFFICULTY

Defeat a series in Expert difficulty to unlock Master difficulty for that series.

FIGHTING COMET

Defeat every series on the Master Class difficulty.

JET VERMILION

Defeat each racing series on Master difficulty with each machine, or defeat the championship 255 times.

FIREPRO WRESTLING

EXTRA WRESTLERS

Select **Edit/Edit Wrestler**, then select **Name Entry**. Enter ALL in the first line. Use the R and L Buttons to move between lines. Enter **STYLE** on the left side of the second line, and **CLEAR** on the right. Set Exchange to Off and Middle to the Square—this is the default. Press **START** and then back up to the main menu. All of the wrestlers should now be selectable.

GT ADVANCE CHAMPIONSHIP RACING

EXTRA MODE 1 (MINI CARS)

At the title screen, hold **L + R** and press **Right + B**.

EXTRA MODE 2 (F1 CAR)

At the title screen, hold **L + R** and press **Left + B**.

CONTINUED

CREDITS

At the title screen, hold **L** + **R** and press
Up + **B**.

ALL TRACKS

At the title screen, hold **L** + **R** and press
Up/Right + **B**.

ALL CARS

At the title screen, hold **L** + **R** and press
Up/Left + **B**.

ALL TUNE UPS

At the title screen, hold **L** + **R** and press
Down/Right + **B**.

GO-KART MODE ALTERNATE METHOD

**Defeat Beginners, Middle, and High-speed in
Championship mode.**

F1 MODE ALTERNATE METHOD

**Defeat all four classes in Championship Mode.
You need to get 1st place in each race.**

IRIDION 3D

ALL LEVELS

Enter ***SH0WT1M3*** as a password.

GALLERY OF RENDERS

Enter ***G4LL3RY*** as a password.

PASSWORDS

STAGE	PASSWORD
2	BKMBVNG7L
3	BVOBBFGCH
4	D9DCBYZ7C
5	OLVCVYQGD
6	8M9CVYV3D
7	XVPDBP6FF

KONAMI KRAZY RACERS

UNLOCK BEAR TANK

Select the Cyber Field 2 course in any mode except Free Race. Grab the blue diamond just before the finish line. Complete the race.

UNLOCK KING

Select the Sky Bridge 2 course in any mode except Free Race. You will need to make a big jump to the right at the first large gap. You may land on a platform with a blue diamond. Pick it up and complete the race.

UNLOCK VIC VIPER

Select the Moon Road course in any mode except Free Race. At the first big gap, make a big jump to the right. You may land on a platform with a blue diamond. Pick it up and complete the race.

UNLOCK EBISUMARU

Use Bear Tank to break the records on Ganbare Dochu 1 and 2.

LEGEND OF ZELDA: ORACLE OF SEASONS

LOCKED SHOP

In Oracle of Seasons, you will find a building in the village with two doors. Playing this game on the Game Boy Color, the right door will be locked. If you play this title on a Game Boy Advance, the shop will be open.

PITFALL: THE MAYAN ADVENTURE

ALL LEVELS, ALL WEAPONS, MOVE ANYWHERE

At the title screen, press **L, SELECT, A, SELECT, R, A, L, SELECT**.

Use **SELECT** and **R or L** to highlight a level. Press **Left** to choose that level.

Hold **SELECT** and press the **B Button** during a game to get 99 of each weapon.

Hold **SELECT** and press in any direction during a game to move in that direction.

START AT LAKAMUL RAIN FOREST

Press **A, L, A, R, A, L, SELECT, SELECT, START** at the title screen.

9 CONTINUES

At the continue screen, repeatedly press **START**.

READY 2 RUMBLE BOXING ROUND 2

MICHAEL JACKSON

At the main menu, highlight Arcade and press **Left, Left, Right, Right, Left, Right, L + R**.

CONTINUED

SHAQ

At the main menu, highlight Survival and press **Left(4), Right, Right, Left, Left, Right, L + R.**

RUMBLEMAN

At the main menu, highlight Championship and press **Left, Left, Right, Left, Right, Right, Left, Right, Left, L + R.**

SUPER DODGE BALL ADVANCE

SPECIAL CHAMPIONSHIP

Defeat Rocket team in the finals of Championship mode.

DREAM TEAMS

Unlock the Dream Teams by defeating the Championship and Special Championship modes.

WORLD 1-3 WARP TO WORLD 4

Keep moving to the right, past the exit door, until you find this Vase. There's a Coin above it, so make the super-jump and grab it!

If you put a potion down here (at the end of this area on the right), you can jump into the jar and warp directly to World 4!

WORLD 3-1 WARP TO WORLD 5

After grabbing the second Ace Coin, move back to the center and land on the island. Use the Magic Potion here to get some coins and a mushroom, or access the warp to World 5.

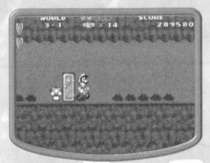

CONTINUED

A
B
C
D
E
F
G
H
I
J
K
L
M
N
O
P
Q
R
S
T
U
V
W
X
Y
Z

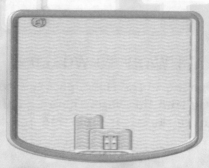

WORLD 4-2 WARP TO WORLD 6

Bring a Potion over to this inaccessible Jar to open a doorway to Subspace. Entering the Jar will now warp you directly to World 6!

WORLD 5-3 WARP TO WORLD 7

First go to the area directly above the ladder. If you're Luigi, you can do this by doing a Super Jump. If you're Mario or one of the other characters, you must climb on a shell and jump from there.

There's a Subspace Warp in this Jar that takes you to World 7.

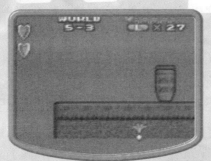

SLEEP MODE

Press **SELECT** + R. Press **SELECT** + L to awaken the GBA.

TONY HAWK'S PRO SKATER 2

SPIDER-MAN

At the main menu or while paused during a game, hold **R** and press **Up, Up, Down, Down, Left, Right, Left, Right, B, A, START**.

SPIDER-MAN WALL CRAWL

At the main menu or while paused during a game, hold **R** and press **Right, A, Down, B, A, START, Down, A, Right, Down**. Do a Wall Ride and Spidey will continue up the wall. Be careful, this may lock up your GBA!

ALL LEVELS AND MAXIMUM MONEY

At the main menu or while paused during a game, hold **R** and press **B, A, Left, Down, B, Left, Up, B, Up, Left, Left**.

A
B
C
D
E
F
G
H
I
J
K
L
M
N
O
P
Q
R
S
T
U
V
W
X
Y
Z

ALL LEVELS

At the main menu or while paused during a game, hold **R** and press **A**, **START**, **A**, **Right**, **Up**, **Up**, **Down**, **Down**, **Up**, **Up**, **Down**.

REPLACE BLOOD WITH FACES

At the main menu, hold **R** and press **START**, **A**, **Down**, **B**, **A**, **Left**, **Left**, **A**, **Down**.

ZOOM IN AND OUT

Pause the game, hold **R** and press **Left**, **A**, **START**, **A**, **Right**, **START**, **Right**, **Up**, **START**.

ALL CHEATS

At the main menu or while paused during a game, hold **R** and press **B**, **A**, **Down**, **A**, **START**, **START**, **B**, **A**, **Right**, **B**, **Right**, **A**, **Up**, **Left**. You will find the cheats in the Options menu.

NO TIME LEFT

At the main menu or while paused during a game, hold **R** and press **Left**, **Up**, **START**, **Up**, **Right**.

NO BLOOD

At the main menu or while paused during a game, hold **R** and press **B**, **Left**, **Up**, **Down**, **Left**, **START**, **START**. Re-enter the code to turn the blood back on.

LEGAL INFO

GAME BOY®

Game Boy® is a registered trademark of Nintendo of America Inc.

102 DALMATIONS: PUPPIES TO THE RESCUE developed by Disney Interactive/Crystal Dynamics/Digital Eclipse, published by Activision. All rights reserved.

1942 developed by Digital Eclipse, published by Capcom. All rights reserved.

ACTION MAN © ©2001 Infogrames Interactive, Inc. All Rights Reserved Used With Permission ©2001 THQ Inc. All Rights Reserved.

ARMY MEN ©2001 The 3DO Company All rights reserved.

ARMY MEN 2 ©2001 The 3DO Company All rights reserved.

ARMY MEN: AIR COMBAT ©2001 The 3DO Company All rights reserved.

ARMY MEN: SARGE'S HEROES 2 ©2001 The 3DO Company All rights reserved.

ASTERIX: SEARCH FOR DOGMATIX ©2000 Infogrames Interactive, Inc. All Rights Reserved.

ASTEROIDS Developed by Syrox Developments Ltd. Published by Activision. All rights reserved.

AUSTIN POWERS: OH BEHAVE! © 2000 Rockstar Games. All Rights Reserved.

AUSTIN POWERS: WELCOME TO MY UNDERGROUND LAIR! © 2000 Rockstar Games. All Rights Reserved.

AZURE DREAMS ©2000 Konami. Konami is a registered trademark of Konami Co., Ltd. All rights reserved.

BABE AND FRIENDS © 2000 Crave Entertainment, Inc. All Rights Reserved.

BATMAN BEYOND: CHAOS IN GOTHAM ©2000 KEMCO. Batman Beyond is the property of DC Comics. TM and ©1999 DC Comics. All rights reserved.

BEAT MANIA GB2: GOTCHA MIX ©2000 Konami. Konami is a registered trademark of Konami Co., Ltd. All Rights Reserved.

BILLY BOB'S HUNTIN' 'N' FISHIN' ©2000 Midway Home Entertainment Inc. All rights reserved.

BLADE developed by HAL Corp. and Avit Inc., published by Activision. All rights reserved.

BLASTER MASTER: ENEMY BELOW Published by Sunsoft. All rights reserved.

BOARDER ZONE ™ & © 2000 Infogrames. Boarder Zone and Infogrames are trademarks or registered trademarks of Infogrames North America, Inc.

BOMBERMAN MAX BLUE CHAMPION/RED CHALLENGER Developed by Hudson. Published by Vatical Entertainment. All rights reserved.

BUFFY THE VAMPIRE SLAYER © 2000 Twentieth Century Fox Film Corporation. All Rights Reserved. Published and distributed by THQ Inc. © 2000 THQ Inc. All Rights Reserved.

BUGS BUNNY CRAZY CASTLE 4 ©2000 KEMCO. Licensed by Nintendo. All rights reserved.

BUZZ LIGHTYEAR OF STAR COMMAND ©Disney/Pixar. Activision is a registered trademark of Activision, Inc. ©2000 Activision, Inc. All rights reserved.

CATWOMAN developed by Kemco Japan, Published by Kemco. All rights reserved.

CHICKEN RUN © 2000 THQ Inc. All Rights Reserved.

CONKER'S POCKET TALES Developed by Rare. Published by Nintendo. All rights reserved.

CROC ©2000 Argonaut Software Ltd. All rights reserved. Croc is a trademark of Argonaut Software Ltd.

DAFFY DUCK: THE MARVIN MISSIONS Looney Tunes, characters, names, and all related indicia are trademarks of Warner Bros. ©1994 Sunsoft. All rights reserved.

GAME BOY® ADVANCE